NIK FILTERS: SUDDEN SERVICE

By Richard Baker

Hello. You're welcome to read this book as many times as you'd like, and I hope you enjoy it. Keep in mind, though, that it is copyright © 2014 by Richard H. Baker (that's me), and I reserve all rights to it. Please don't make copies or transmit it to someone else, regardless of how you do it. If you do that, I have the right to raise a stink about it. I'd be glad if you recommend it to other folks, but they should buy their own copies. This book doesn't cost that much.

Officially, this book is published by Baker Publications, which is another name I go by. Unlike so many other publishers these days, it is not a division of anything else.

I'd add some Library of Congress catalog data here, except that the Library of Congress hasn't gotten around to cataloging it.

Contents

Introduction

Rural diners used to post signs promising "Sudden Service." Some probably still do. This book is intended to offer much the same thing: quick access to help you get an immediate job done using the NIK filters. You can read it end to end. But you'll often find it more useful as a handy reference to help you get the most from the NIK filters. In fact, you can carry this book in electronic form, right on the iPad itself.

Check the contents or the index for the job you need to do; then, you can jump directly to that section. Cross-references lead you to other helpful information.

Chapter 1. Getting acquainted

The NIK Collection is a group of half a dozen applications you can use to edit and improve your photographs. Though they can function as stand-alone applications, they most often work as plug-ins to other photo editing applications like Photoshop, Aperture, or Lightroom.

The European firm of NIK Software developed these applications. Now in the hands of Google, they are available as the NIK Collection, which is made up of:

- Dfine 2, which you can use to control the electronic "noise" that crops up in many images.

- Viveza 2, which controls light and color.

- HDR Efex Pro 2, which turns a series of bracketed exposures into a single High Dynamic Range picture with a range of exposure you can't normally achieve in a single photograph.

- Color Efex Pro 4, which as its name suggests, applies a variety of color effects.

- Silver Efex Pro 2, which turns color images into black and white photos.

- Sharpener Pro 3, which applies two types of sharpening: capture sharpening to reduce the softness that naturally occurs in a digital image, and output sharpening which applies sharpening to match the intended use of the image.

Probably the distinguishing feature of this collection is its U Point technology. This is a selection tool with which you select a specific point in the image. Then, you can expand or contract a circle around that point and apply changes specifically to items within that circle.

For more on using U Point, see "3. Pointing with U Point".

1. Open a filter

Lightroom and Aperture are competing products that for the most part do the same things in much the same ways. That includes serving as host applications for the NIK filters.

Each of these applications displays an array of photos, sorted into folders or similar subdivisions, and searchable by keywords. Find the picture you want to edit, select it, and invoke the filter you want to use.

These are professional-level products whose features complement in many ways the NIK filters. Their interfaces differ—one 's by Apple, the other by Adobe—but even allowing for the vast array of functions each offers, you'll probably find them easy to use. They organize images in sensible fashion, particularly if you want to open multiple images for High Dynamic Range (HDR) processing.

There are some drawbacks. If you expect the layers and smart filters found in Photoshop, you won't find them here. Similarly, there's no provision for batch processing.

The other option for opening the filters is to do so through Photoshop. This graphic arts creator is an art medium in its own right. Opening the filter through Photoshop gives you this venerable program's ful range of options and features.

Open a filter from Lightroom

Lightroom gives you several ways to select a picture to edit. You can work with a copy of the picture with any modifications you have made in Lightroom, a copy without the modifications, or the original file. You'll make this choice when you open the picture in the NIK plug-in.

To start, right-click on the picture, and select **Edit In**. A variety of editing options is displayed, including the NIK plug-ins.

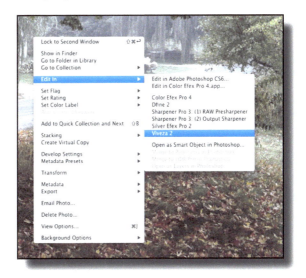

Select the filter you want to use. You then are asked to select the type of image you want to edit.

Make your choice. If you choose to make a copy , go to the lower half and enter your specifications for that copy. Click on **Edit**, and the picture opens in the selected plug-in.

Sometimes, Lightroom does limit your choices here. For example, if you have saved your pictures in DNG format, your only choice is to open the picture with Lightroom adjustments.

Open a filter from Aperture

Right-click on the picture you want to edit. This can be either a thumbnail or the full loupe display. Select **Edit with Plug-in.** The NIK plug-ins are displayed along with any other plug-ins you might have installed.

Apple purists would claim the proper instruction is to Control-click. It has been many years, though, since Apple produced a mouse without a right-click function.

Click on the plug-in you want to use. The picture opens in that plug-in.

When you finish editing in the plug-in, the program will save a new or revised version of the picture.

Open a filter from Photoshop

Photoshop is the most versatile program from which to implement a NIK plug-in. It is, of course, a top-rank graphic editor and offers probably the greatest variety of features and functions you can find. When you use Photoshop with a NIK plug-in, all its features, like layers and smart filters, are available as well.

Smart Filters can be a particularly valuable resource when working with the plug-ins. They let you make nondestructive edits in Photoshop much like you can make in Aperture and Lightroom. Should you want to alter your changes at any time, including removing them entirely, you can readily do so.

You also can use Photoshop tools like the Lasso, Magic Wand, and Paths to selectively apply the NIK plug-ins to selected parts of the photo. Should you need the advanced power of 32-bit images, Photoshop can handle these.

All this makes Photoshop the most extensive—and expensive—platform; its advanced features come at a price. Its files tend to grow rapidly, particularly if you use layers. It's also a notorious memory hog.

One way to reduce the cost is to use its junior version, Photoshop Elements. Designed mainly for photo management, Elements has many features of the senior product. That includes the ability to position the output of a NIK plug-in as a separate layer so you can edit nondestructively. On the other hand, Elements lacks smart filters, it cannot do batch processing, and it also might have some high memory demands.

To open a NIK filter in Photoshop, click on the picture you want to edit. If you want to use a smart filter, select **Filter > Convert for Smart Filters**.

You then have two choices for opening a plug-in. The most direct is to select **Filter > NIK Collection**. The available plug-ins appear in a sub-menu.

The other, more versatile, choice is to use the *Selective Tool* that appears in the lower right-hand corner of the screen.

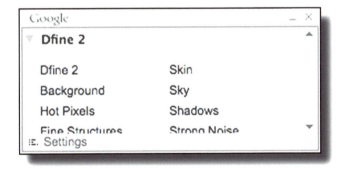

If you look closely, as you must, you'll see that the tool displays all the available NIK filters as well as any presents that have been applied to them. Click on your choice.

At the bottom of the Selective Tool is a **Settings** button you can use to manage the tool's operation. A dialog box gives you a choice of settings, including whether to apply the filter to a layer or to the base picture.

From Elements, the procedure is much the same. You have no Smart Filters option, but you can open the plug-ins by selecting **Filters > NIK Collection**.

As in Photoshop, the Selective Tool is available along with its Settings menu.

2. What's on the screen?

Each of the NIK plug-ins has its unique features, and their on-screen appearance varies accordingly. Nevertheless, the individual plug-ins look and work much alike. For example, the Viveza screen looks much like the screens for the other plug-ins.

Like the other plug-ins, it has a large image area, a toolbar across the top, another at the bottom, and a right-hand panel with controls that are specific to the product.

The top toolbar

Some NIK filters have left-hand panels that feature preset filters you can apply to the image.

At the left-hand end of the top toolbar are buttons that control the display. A group of **Views** buttons let you control the way your adjustments are displayed.

The first, solid, button displays your adjustments on the entire image. The middle button splits the picture; one side displays the original image; the other your changes.

The third button displays the original and your adjustments as separate pictures.

The **Preview** check box lets you decide whether to display your changes at all.

At the right-hand end of this toolbar is a collection of tools that let you do things like zoom in and out, make selections, and change the background color of the image area. Tool tips describe each of them.

Across the bottom

The bottom toolbar provides buttons for use when operating the program, like calling for help and saving your work.

The right-hand windows

At the right is a panel of windows that exercise the basic functions of the specific plug-in. For example, this window displays sliders for adjusting brightness, contrast, and other settings.

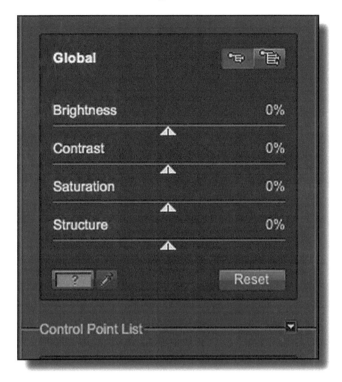

Also in this panel is a loupe display that compares a section of the original image with the edited version. Point to the area in the picture you want to compare.

3. Pointing with U Point

Probably the most distinctive feature of the NIK plug-ins is the U Point system. To use it, place a *control point* on the part of a picture you want to edit. Then use sliders to apply changes. These changes apply only to the areas of the picture that are managed by the control point.

For example, in this picture, the sun-lit portions of the wall are slightly burned-out and lack detail. You can change these without affecting the exposure of the rest of the picture.

There are several ways to do this; Color Efex offers a quick, simple solution. In the **Control Points** window, click on the Control Points symbol with a + (plus) sign.

A control point appears at that location. You can drag it around if you wish.

This particular control point has two sliders. The upper one controls the area the control point will govern. Slide it back and forth, and a circle describes the area it will affect. Adjust the U Point to cover at least most of the overexposed area. Any change you apply now will take effect only within this area.

A right-hand panel displays sliders that match those on the U Point. Use the **Brightness** slider to reduce the exposure of the selected area.

The picture now shows more detail in this area.

More options

Some other plug-ins have a greater range of effects. For example, in Viveza a control point shows sliders to control brightness, contrast, saturation and structure.

Applying U Point

Structure is a NIK feature you can use to emphasize or smooth details.

The NIK plug-ins use control points to control the specific effects of each product. The Size slider is universal, but otherwise the control points vary with the product.

Control points are selection tools; they define the area to which an effect will be applied.

In the earlier example, Color Efex used only size and opacity sliders. Viveza, the most versatile of the NIK products, showed sliders for brightness, contrast, saturation and structure. You also can use Viveza control points to adjust the three RGB colors, red, green, and blue, plus warmth and hue.

Silver Efex provides similar sliders, but they are geared to black-and-white pictures.

In Dfine, control points provide sliders to apply noise reduction. In HDR Efex you can use sliders to selectively adjust exposure. The Sharpener plug-ins let you increase or reduce the sharpening of different regions.

Chapter 2. Defining with Dfine

If you're going to apply more than one NIK plug-in to a picture, there's a generally accepted sequence, or workflow, for doing so. The exact order depends on which of the plug-ins you plan to use, but most often Dfine is the starting point.

While most of the collection is designed to help you enhance an image, Dfine is positioned as a problem-solver. It makes sense, then, to use it at the outset so the problems don't remain to complicate your efforts to make things better. The problem Dfine attacks is called *digital noise*. It's the grainy effect that often crops up in what are otherwise supposed to be areas of continuous color.

In many ways, digital noise mimics the earliest form of photographic noise, which was *film grain*. That was caused by clumps of silver that made up the film's light-sensitive elements. The higher the film's ISO rating, the more pronounced the grain.

Digital noise emulates film grain; in many Ways. It shows up most often in dark areas when the camera was set to a high ISO. Visible *artifacts* are electronic counterparts to the clumps of film grain.

Digital noise shows up as variations in what should be a smooth area. It can appear in either of two forms:

Ironically, Silver Efex, the collection's tool for black and white photography makes it possible to reproduce those old films, including their grain.

- Contrast noise, or more technically *luminance noise*. It appears as variations in the same color.

- Color, or *chrominance*, noise which takes the form of unwanted colored specks.

The most obvious use of Dfine is to smooth out visible noise that distracts from the intended effect of a photo. You can get rid of the noise in a full image, or you can use control points to apply it to selected parts of the photo. For example, you could use Dfine to smooth the skin in a portrait.

There are many situations, though, where the noise doesn't become apparent until after you have done some editing of the image. Even though the noise is not immediately apparent, it is a good idea to apply Dfine in situations like these:

- You expect to brighten all or part of the picture.

- You expect to make significant changes in the contrast.

- You expect to convert the image to black and white.

- You want to preserve the grungy effect that often characterizes HDR photos.

4. Measure noise

The first step in getting rid of noise is to find out how much noise you actually have. When you start the program, it does this automatically. For example, this photo shows a variety of rocks, trees and grass; none of these is a good candidate for noise measurement and reduction. But it does have a patch of relatively uniform sky.

The noise here may not be immediately visible, but any noise that does exist could show up as you edit the picture further.

Open the program

When you open the photo in Dfine, the program zooms in on this area of sky and draws a rectangle there.

Dfine automatically measures the noise within the rectangle and creates a noise reduction profile for this picture. It will use this profile to correct the noise in the overall picture.

Refine the measurement

If you wish, you can save this profile and apply it to other pictures.

Dfine generally does a good job of measuring noise from the initial rectangle, but it can do a better job if it has more rectangles to work with. You can add these manually. You also can expand existing rectangles.

To add a rectangle, switch the **Method** from Automatic to Manual. Just below, click on the **Add Rectangle** button.

Then, draw or expand the rectangles on the screen.

Click on **Measure Noise.** The program recalculates the noise and writes a new profile.

5. Reduce the noise

Now that you've assessed any noise in the picture, you are in a better position to reduce it effectively.

Dfine provides two paths for reducing noise:

- You can reduce noise in the entire document, or:

- You can concentrate your efforts on areas you can select using control points.

To start the process, go to the Control Panel, and click on **Reduce**. If you want to use control points, select this as the **Method**.

Sliders give you the means to control both contrast and color noise. If you have established one or more control points, these settings are applied to them. Otherwise, they are applied to the entire picture.

Adjust the noise

Each slider begins at a setting of 100 percent, which again is useful for most images. Increasing a slider setting further reduces noise, but it might also reduce detail in the picture. Decreasing a slider setting does just the opposite.

In this case, the slider adjustments don't have much visible effect smoother areas like the sky and rocks. On the other hand, the trees and grass might require trade-offs between noise control and loss of detail.

Add control points

In such a case, you can add control points to restrict your noise control to selected areas. With the Method set to control points, click on one of the Add Control Point buttons

Then, click in the image where you want the control point to appear.

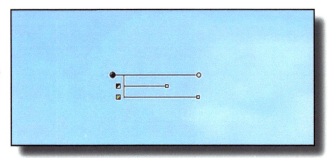

As usual, the upper control point button controls the extent of the area where it is applied. The other two buttons control the kind and amount of noise control that are applied to the selected area.

You can apply additional control points to control other parts of the picture.

6. Control noise in individual colors

You may have an image where noise is most prominent in a particular color. In that case, you can manage the noise only in that color.

Set the **Method** to **Color Ranges**. Sets of sliders open for each color in the Red, Green, Blue set.

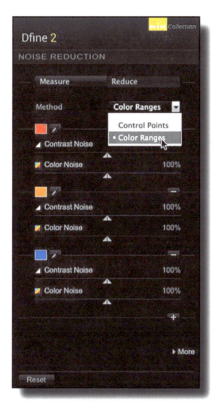

7. Correct specific noise problems

At the bottom of the control panel is a **More** button that opens the way to more specialized controls. You may not need these often, but they're available just in case. Open the **More** list, and check the items you want to apply.

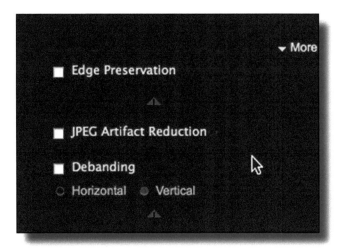

- **Edge Preservation** sharpens edges that might otherwise be blurred by the noise control process. A slider lets you control the effect.

- **JPEG Artifact Reduction** reduces the square artifacts that sometimes show up in compressed JPEG images.

- **Debanding** reduces the colored bands digital cameras sometimes produce.

8. Brush out noise

A central purpose of the selective tools is the ability to brush on noise controls using Photoshop's array of brushes. In this case, you can use Strong Noise to brush out the heavy grain in the back of a car.

Open the file

Open the picture in Photoshop. In the **Selective Tools** window, click on **Strong Noise**. The filter is applied as a new layer, but a solid black mask hides its application.

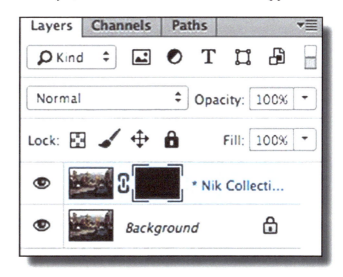

Using the Photoshop display, zoom in on the car at the lower right-hand corner. Its finish shows heavy noise.

In this case, the noise actually is film grain. This is a very old picture.

Select a brush

Make sure the added layer is selected. In the upper left-hand corner of the Photoshop display, select the type of brush you want to use.

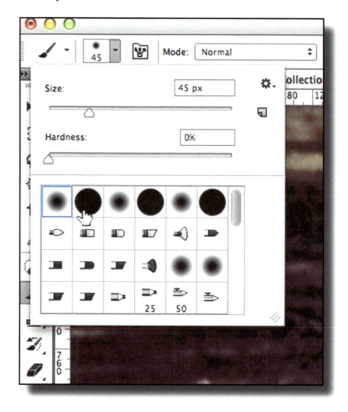

Paint the noise away

A soft, round brush is a good choice for this picture. Use the square bracket keys ([or]) to enlarge or shrink the brush.

Paint the back of the car. As you proceed, the noise is reduced. It may take several passes to reduce this heavy noise to the level you want.

9. Apply selective tools

You may note that as you reduce noise, you also reduce the readability of the license plate. This is the usual trade-off between sharpness and noise reduction.

If you start Dfine from Photoshop or Photoshop Elements, you have some extra noise-reducing tools. These are available in the Selective Tools window along with similar options for other members of the collection.

The Dfine tools include:

- **Dfine** itself, which you can apply to the overall image or brush it onto selected areas.

- **Background**, which you can use to control noise in the background of the picture.

- **Hot Pixels** can control bright noise spots that sometimes appear in dark areas.

- **Fine Structures** is useful when you need to maintain a balance between noise control and fine detail such as hair.

- **Skin**. Useful for smoothing skin, again while maintaining some detail.

- **Sky**. Reduces type types of noise that often appear in the sky.

- **Shadows**. Manage the noise in dark areas of the picture.

- **Strong Noise.** Use this to control particularly noisy pictures.

Apply Dfine

Since these are called selective tools, the basic intent is that you brush these effects onto particular areas of the picture.

If you open the picture in Photoshop or Elements, in the main menu, you can select **Filters > Convert for Smart Filters**. In the **Selective Tools** window, click on **Dfine 2.0**.

The picture opens in Dfine and begins the automatic measurement and noise reduction process described in *"4. Measure noise"*. Three buttons appear in the Navigator window.

Click on **OK**. The edited picture reopens in Photoshop.

If you select Brush,
you can use Photoshop
brushes to apply Dfine
to selected areas of the
photo.

The Layers window shows that the changes have been added in the form of a smart layer.

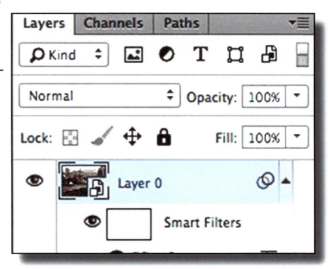

You now can use that layer to brush on Dfine changes in the areas that need them.

10. Soften skin

In the process of removing noise, Dfine also can have a softening effect on skin. In particular, you can use the Skin selective tool to soften the skin in portraits, apart from its value in removing noise.

Open the picture in Photoshop

This photo, taken in bright sunshine, creates some harshness around the model's features.

Select a brush

From the Selective Tools list, select **Skin**. In Photoshop, select a soft brush. Use the [or] keys to make it larger or smaller.

Brush on the effect

Apply the brush to the model's face. The overall appearance will be smoothed out.

Chapter 3. Color Efex

At its heart, Color Efex Pro is a collection of *presets* for managing and controlling the color effects, properly spelled, within a picture.

There are a lot of these, 55 in all. Plus, you can stack multiple presets, use control points to apply them selectively, and even invent your own.

At various times, these presets are also called filters, recipes or plug-ins. *Presets* seems to the most common use.

To reduce the confusion a little, these presets are grouped into *categories*, which more or less display particular presets for particular purposes. The basic technique is to identify the filter that does the job and apply it to your picture.

In practice, you can identify and use the presets that best suit your needs, eventually becoming familiar with some of the others. There's no need to master all 55 at once or even at all.

11. The Color Efex screen

If you're used to using Lightroom or any of several other photo editing applications, the screen should look familiar. The picture occupies the central position. To the left is a list of available presets. To the right is a panel of adjustment options you can use within the selected filter.

35

Compress the list

It these panels are blank, click on the tiny arrows in the upper corners of the display

The full list of all available presets is a bit intimidating, but you can reduce the volume by selecting one of the categories in the upper left-hand corner of the screen. For example, selecting **Landscape**, a natural choice for this picture, reduces the list considerably.

Personalize the list

The categories were chosen for you, but you can arrange them so those you use most are high on the list. The **All** and **Favorites** categories will always share the top row, but you can select which categories appear in order below them.

To change the arrangement, click on the **Settings** button at the bottom of the panel. This opens a dialog box in which you can change the order. When the dialog box opens, click on **Filterlist Settings**.

Then, open the list for each position, and select the preset you want to appear there.

Play Favorites

You can establish one custom category by adding presets to the **Favorites** group. To do this, click on the star next to the category you want to add.

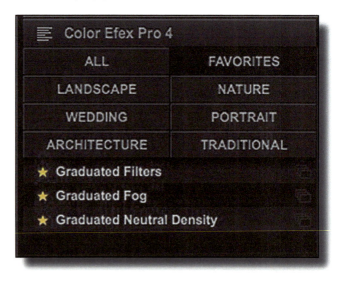

12. Apply a basic filter

This picture is in serious need of a graduated neutral density filter. It's too light at the top and too dark at the bottom.

Set the specifications

When you select the filter, its controls appear in the right-hand panel.settings

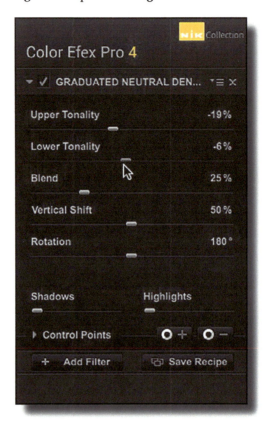

Use the sliders to control the filter's effects. For example, sliding the **Upper Tonality** slider to the left darkens the sky and the sunlit land area.

Lighten the foreground

That still leaves the problem of a foreground that is too dark. To cure this, slide the **Lower Tonality** slider to the right.

Other controls

There are several other controls you can use to govern the effects of this filter. They include:

- **Blend** controls the way the two tonality sliders interact. Slide it to the right, and the darkening effect slips lower into the picture.

- **Vertical Shift** does much the same thing. It controls how far down the filter effect reaches into the picture.

- **Rotation** lets you fit the filter to an uneven horizon.

- **Shadows** and **Highlights** let you modify the bright and dark areas.

As with other NIK presets, you have the option of setting control points to localize the filter's action.

13. Apply multiple presets

You can apply more than one filter at a time, combining the effects of all.

Build a stack

Normally, when you select a new filter from the list, it displaces any other presets that might otherwise be applied.

Nevertheless, you can *stack* presets to apply the effects of all. To add a filter to one already in effect, click on the **Add Filter** button at the bottom of the first filter's control panel.

Then, you can select another filter from the list. The right-hand panel displays controls for both presets. If you expand one filter's controls, the other group is collapsed.

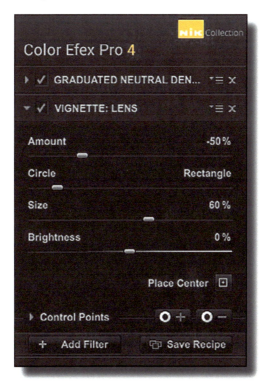

Apply the new filter

In this case, the new set of controls created a vignette around the photo. You can alter this effect to darken or lighten the effect.

Sometimes, you may want to use this effect for its own sake. At other times, you may lighten the vignetted area to compensate for the effects of a camera lens. In this case, it lightened the border areas. This was done by reducing the **Amount** setting.

Other Vignette settings include:

- **Circle/Rectangle**. Apply a more circular or rectangular vignette.

- **Size**. As you probably expect, make the vignette larger or smaller.

- **Brightness**. Again naturally, lighten or darken the effect.

14. Cook up a recipe

Low in the left-hand panel is a **Recipes** button. Click on it, and you will see several preset combinations of effects you can apply to the current picture.

If you have a combination of presets and custom settings you might want to use again, you can create your own recipe.

Apply the effects you want to use. Then, at the bottom of the control group, click on **Save Recipe**. You are asked to enter a name for the recipe. Do so; then, click on **OK**. The recipe is now available in the left-hand panel.

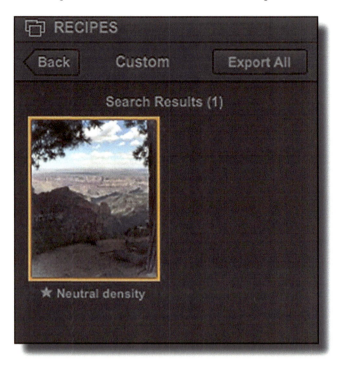

Organize recipes

Click on **Back**. You see a group of recipe categories. The newly added recipe is in the **Custom** group. The display that appeared initially is under **Sample Recipes**.

To add a recipe to the **Favorites**, go to its current location, and click on the star before its name.

15. Browsing through history

The History Browser is a detailed log of each change you have made to the picture. Using this list, you can go back and select any of the previous states to reexamine that step's results. If you like that effect as the final version, you can save the picture in that state.

Compare effects

Perhaps more valuable is the ability to compare two versions.

In the upper left-hand area of the Toolbar, click on **Compare**. The original image is displayed and is flagged in the History Browser.

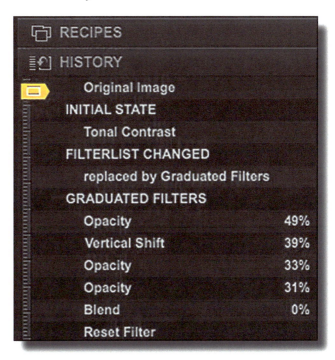

Then, click on the state you'd like to compare.

The two versions open for your inspection.

In the Toolbar, select the Split Screen or Side-by-Side display option to display the two versions.

Chapter 4. Viveza

Viveza is probably the most versatile, and the most complex, of the NIK filter collection. Its main purpose in life is to give you control over the lighting of your photograph.

The basic set of adjustments lets you control brightness, contrast, saturation and structure. An expanded set lets you brighten shadows, add warmth, and adjust the intensity of individual colors.

16. What's on the screen

The basic Viveza screen includes a large space to display the picture and a right-hand control panel to hold the individual controls.

You can use these controls to make global changes that affect the entire picture. Viveza's greatest strength, though,is to make local adjustments using control points.

The Control Panel

Near the top of the Control Panel are the basic
adjustments

For example, to lighten this gloomy, underexposed picture, you can move the sliders, particularly **Brightness**, to the right.

Press **E** to expand the list of available adjustments. You can apply any—or all—of these.

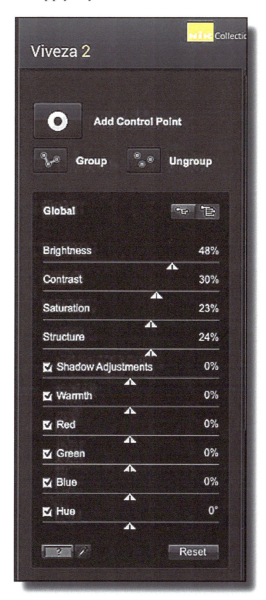

17. Apply curves and levels

Curves and levels were the original basic tools for adjusting brightness and contrast in Photoshop. They're still available in Photoshop and many other image editing applications, including Viveza.

To display them, scroll downward in the Control Panel.

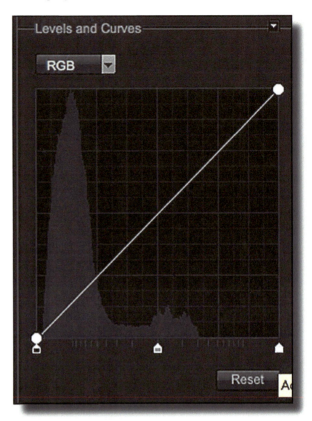

Check the end points

The histogram is a bit dim in this display, but it charts the distribution of tonal values in the picture. In this case, large numbers of darker values are clustered to the left-hand side of the graph; smaller numbers of lighter values appear on the right.

One of the most common uses of this display is to look for instances where extreme light or dark values are off the chart; an indication that they have not been accurately recorded.

Here, there is the opposite problem: light values that fall a little short of the right-hand side of the graph. That's a sign they have not been recorded brightly enough.

At the bottom of the graph, there are three pointers, representing the dark, middle, and bright points. At the right-hand side, nudge the bright pointer to the left until it is beneath the low point of the graph.

This should brighten the picture somewhat.

Adjust the curve

The steeper the curve, the greater the contrast. That has traditionally been the basic principle of curves management. In practice, most pictures can be improved by plotting a slightly S-shaped curve.

Click on the curve toward its left-hand end, and drag it slightly downward. Then, click near the right-hand end and push it slightly upward. This darkens the darks, brightens the lights, and adds contrast to the middle tones.

18. Add control points

If any of the NIK filters is made for control points, it is Viveza. In fact, Viveza encourages multiple control points which can be grouped to make similar adjustments at various places in the picture.

Add a control point

For the basics of using control points, see "3. Pointing with U Point."

At the top of the Control Panel, click on **Add Control Point**. Then, click at the point in the picture where you want the control point to appear

Adjust the point's coverage are by moving the upper arm.

Set the sliders

It may be necessary to press **Ctrl** or **Command**.

You can adjust the settings within the control point by moving either the sliders on the control point itself or the comparable sliders in the Control Panel. The adjustments will affect similar colors within the control point area.

19. Add more control points

In this case, the first control point affected mainly the green tones in the upper left-hand part of the image. You can add a second control point to regulate another color, such as the blue of the river in the lower part of the picture.

You can adjust the sliders to add brightness to this area.

A window below the sliders in the Control Panel indicates the color setting.

20. Group control points

You can group two or more control points to simultaneously control two or more control points. When you do this, you can apply the same adjustments to multiple colors.

Select the points

In the Control Point List, select the control points you want to group.

Near the top of the Control Panel, click on **Group**.

The Control Point List now shows the group. A single set of controls is displayed. They affect all control points in the group.

Adjusting the sliders affects both areas governed by the control points.

The second control
point in the group
does display a size
control. You can
use it to change the
coverage area of that
control point.

21. Pick colors to manage

The color picker in the Control Panel gives you a couple
of additional ways to determine the colors that are
managed by a control point.

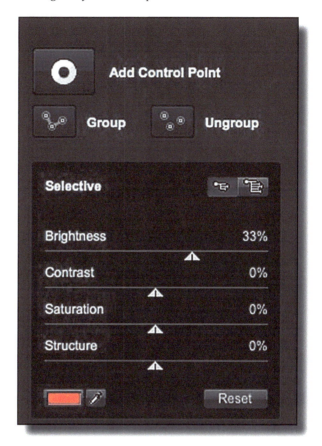

You can use the Eyedropper tool to select a color from
the picture, or you can open the Color Picker and select a
color there.

Select a color

In this picture, the primary object, the truck, is surrounded by numerous distractions, including two people whose shirts are bright primary colors,, red and blue.

You can use control points to desaturate these colors and make them less distracting.

Start by placing a control point on the red shirt. Then, in the Control Panel, select the eyedropper color picker. Use it to click on the shirt.

The control point reflects that color. You can adjust the sliders to reduce the red shade's brightness and saturation.

Pick a color

You can also use the Color Picker to accomplish the same thing. In this picture, you could place a control point on the blue shirt in the upper left. Then, click on the color window.

The color picker opens. Since the offending shirt is a
basic blue, you can select the Blue option.

Close the color picker, and adjust the brightness and saturation of this control point.

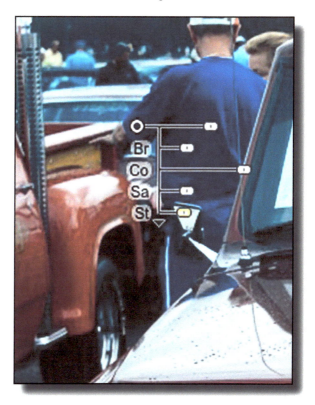

You could group these control points and adjust both at the same time. You also could establish a control point using the color of the truck and brighten its appearance.

Chapter 5. Silver Efex

Ansel Adams worked primarily in black and white. So did the classic photojournalists of *Life* magazine.

Since their respective heydays, color has pretty much taken over—except that black and white has recent enjoyed a revival.

Part of that is due to the emergence of digital photography. Many image editing applications have the ability to render a digital photo in black and white. Silver Efex Pro is one of these, and it enjoys a reputation as one of the best.

Black and white photography differs from color in one important respect: instead of viewing the effects of various colors, you see the effects of various shades of light and darkness. This can add a whole new artistic dimension to your work as you adjust the shading of various parts of the image.

22. What's on the screen?

The Silver Effects screen is—no surprise—a variation on the overall theme of the NIK plug-ins.

In the left-hand panel is a group of preset filters. You can use these to apply standard combinations of light and shade. In the right-hand panel are custom adjustments you can use to tailor the shading exactly.

23. Apply preset filters

The left-hand panel is dominated by the preset filters you can use to quickly apply effects to a picture.

Scroll down, if necessary, to find an effect you want.
Click on it, and it is immediately applied to the picture.

Organize the filters

You can use these
presets as starting
points for custom
adjustments.

At the top of the filter panel is a list of classifications
that narrow down the selection. For the most part, the
classifications have been made for you, but you can
select your own favorites.

To designate a favorite, click on the star before the filter's name.

Invent your own filters

When you have found a series of settings that suits a particular purpose, you can save it as a custom filter.

Use the right-hand panel to make the settings you want. Then, in the left-hand panel, click on the **Plus** sign next to the **Custom** button. You'll be asked to name the new custom filter.

Give it a name, and click on **OK**. Click on **Custom**, and the new filter appears in that group. It contains the settings that were in effect when you started the process.

Reviving history

At the bottom of the left-hand panel, the **History** button opens a list of every change you've made to this picture. Click on any of these steps, and the picture reverts to that point in the process.

24. Adjust brightness and contrast

In the right-hand panel, the upper controls should be familiar: sliders to control brightness, contrast, and that NIK staple, structure.

You can adjust each of these individually to customize the tonal mix of your picture. For example, in this case the picture is too dark and has excessive contrast. You can adjust the sliders to produce a softer tone.

If you want more detail, you can open each of these groups of sliders to apply them to specific tonal areas.

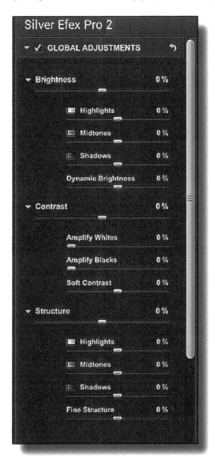

25. Adjust with control points

Once you have found the right combination of settings, you can save them as a custom preset. See "23. Apply preset filters"

Just as with the other NIK filters, you can use control points to make selective adjustments. For instance, you might want to darken the bright area in the bushes at the left-hand side of this picture.

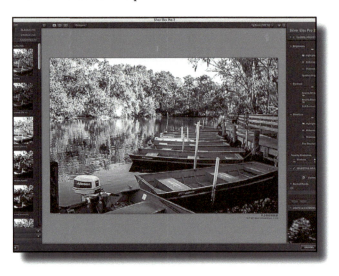

Set up a control point in this area.

Then, adjust the brightness downward until this area is a better match for the rest of the picture.

26. Lighten a selected color

Each color in a color original translates itself into a particular shade in black and white. In this picture, the green of the foreground shrubbery becomes an uncomfortably dark shade. You can use a color selector to adjust the way this color is displayed.

In the **Color Filter** section of the right-hand panel, click on the color you would like to change, in this case green.

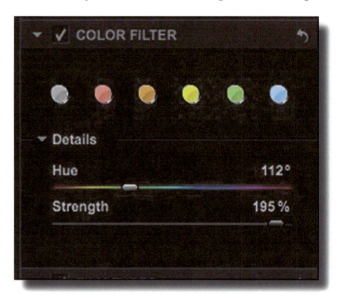

Adjust the **Strength** slider to lighten the shade.

27. Apply the zone system

Ansel Adams popularized the zone system for judging exposure in black and white photography. The zones run from zero, the darkest, to 10, the lightest. Ideally they should show a uniform distribution between all ten zones.

Point your mouse toward the **Loupe & Histogram** window at the bottom of the control panel. Numbers representing the zone system appear along the bottom.

Point to any of these numbers, and crosshatching will show the areas of the picture that fall within that zone.

Chapter 6. Just right sharpening

Sharpening is an essential part of digital photography. Nearly every process, from the light through the camera lens to a final print, induces some softness in the image.

But sharpening is easy to overdo. We probably are all familiar with the over-sharpened photo in which garish halos surround the picture's elements. It is these halos that produce the sharpening effect, but it's all to easy to go overboard.

Photoshop uses the term *unsharp mask,* so-called because it masks areas that are not sharp.

The NIK filters include two sharpening tools: an input sharpener and an output sharpener. They are intended for different stages of the editing process.

The input sharpener, called the *Raw Presharpener,* is one of the first you'll want to use. It corrects for the natural lack of sharpness in the original digital photo.

The NIK output sharpener should be one of the last you use. It sharpens the picture for a specific use such as a printed page or an electronic image.

This kind of sharpening is best applied to raw files. When a camera produces a JPEG file, it automatically adds some sharpening.

Either way, it's important to apply sharpening according to the Goldilocks principle: not too little, not too much, but just right.

28. Input sharpening

The Raw Presharpener is hardly unique. Most picture editors including Photoshop, Lightroom, and Aperture, include sharpening tools of their own. In truth, all do a decent job of sharpening an incoming picture.

The advantage of the Raw Presharpener is that it is a specialized, stand-alone tool that can do a precise job of striking the sharpening balance you need.

Turn off competitors

The first step toward using the NIK presharpener is
to turn off competing products. For example, in the
Lightroom develop module, the amount of sharpening
should equal zero.

Then, you can edit the picture in the Raw Presharpener.

What's on the screen

The sharpener displays the picture along with a right-
hand panel that contains the primary controls.

Across the top of the screen is the usual toolbar, which includes options for displaying the entire photo, a split screen that compares sharpened with unsharpened versions, or two separate versions of the picture.

In the lower right-hand corner, a Loupe section displays a small split screen with enlarged view of the picture. Move the mouse pointer around to display different areas.

Operating the controls

The Presharpener section of the control panel has three main controls:

- **Adaptive Sharpening**. This is comparable to the **Amount** setting in other sharpening products. In Silver Efex, this kicks in at 50%, which is a useful setting for many pictures. Some images may require more or less, so it pays to experiment. Keep an eye on the Loupe to avoid the excess fringing that comes with over-sharpening.

- **Sharpen areas or edges**. With this slider, you can choose to concentrate the sharpening on the edges or on the smoother areas between the edges. Again, the initial setting is 50%, which is an even split between the two targets. Again, it pays to experiment. Usually, a slight tilt toward the edges tends to get noticed more quickly.

- **Image quality**. Digital cameras can operate at much higher ISO settings than their film counterparts. The drawback is that the higher the ISO, the more likely you are to encounter digital noise. If that becomes a problem while sharpening, selecting the **High ISO** setting can help.

See *"Chapter 2. Defining with Dfine"* for more on dealing with noise.

29. Sharpen for output

Output sharpening is a little different. It depends on the use you plan to make of the picture. Sharpening for a large print is different from sharpening for a smaller print or for on-screen display.

What's on the screen

The controls on the right-hand panel reflect the difference between these two types of sharpening. The output sharpener adjusts for various types of output. This panel also has sections for creative and selective sharpening.

Prepare the picture

Before attempting any output sharpening, make sure the picture is otherwise fully adjusted and is the proper size for the intended output.

Select the output

Open the **Output Sharpening** list, and select the output you plan to use.

The choices are:

- **Display**. Use this setting for any kind of computer display or projector. The only control here is **Adaptive Sharpening**. As with the Presharpening filter, it controls the amount of sharpening. The initial setting of 50% is often a good choice.

- **Inkjet**. This is for items printed on an inkjet printer. Here, you can sharpen for a particular viewing distance, paper type and printed size.

The closer a viewer is
to the print, the more
detail is visible.

- **Continuous Tone**. This is the choice for pictures to be printed at a commercial photo lab. Adjustments are available for viewing distance and printer resolution.

- **Halftone**. This is the setting for commercial printing. **Newsprint** is one of the available paper types along with various kinds of coated paper. The printer resolution is pre-set.

- **Hybrid Device**. This could be any combination of the other methods.

30. Refine your sharpening

Once you have set the output specifications, you can use the **Creative Sharpening** section to refine the image.

Apply creative controls

The **Creative Controls** section gives you the means to apply custom sharpening to the image or—using control points—to selected parts of it.

The options are:

- **Output Sharpening Strength** amplifies or dampens the effects of your Output Sharpening settings. You could use this to set global sharpening to zero, then use control points to sharpen selected parts of the picture.

- **Structure** applies the NIK Structure setting to the picture. This is a contrast enhancement tool you can use to emphasize the structure and texture of an image without introducing excessive halos around the edges.

- **Local contrast** applies another type of contrast enhancement. It can help emphasize objects in the picture, but it *can* induce halos, so use it sparingly.

- **Focus** tries to bring out-of-focus items into focus. No software tool can do this completely, but this tool makes a good attempt. It may work best in reverse: apply a negative value to reduce the focus of a background.

31. Apply selective controls

In both the Presharpening and Output Sharpening filters, you have the option of using control points to apply sharpening to selected areas.

For details of using control points, see *"3. Pointing with U Point."*

You can also reduce excess sharpening. For example, in this photo the global sharpening settings went overboard on the dog's fur.

Add a control point with a radius that covers the dog; then, reduce the **Output Sharpening Strength**. The fur now looks more natural.

Display the effect

In the toolbar, there is a drop-down list of **Modes**. There are two you can use to check the effect of a control point.

- **Effect overlay** uses a red overlay to indicate the areas covered by the control point.

- **Effect Mask** applies a white mask to the selected area.

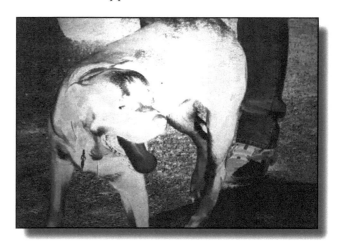

Chapter 7. HDR Efex

One of the first things you may have learned about photographic lighting is that the human eye can see and balance a much wider range of brightness—the so-called *dynamic range*—than any existing film or digital sensor.

The classic example is of a scenic shot in which the land area is properly exposed but the sky is so bright it is washed out. Or, you might have an interior shot in which an area outside a window is excessively bright.

High Dynamic Range imaging, or HDR for short, is one means of dealing with that. It merges a range of exposures into a single image in which all areas are (more or less) properly exposed. HDR Efex conducts that merger.

Consider, for example, a series of exposures that includes an interior room and the sunlit exterior outside a window. One exposure is right for the room but shows only a washed-out exterior. Another exposure is right for the exterior but leaves the interior almost completely dark. Other exposures range between these extremes, but none is right for the entire scene.

HDR Efex can consolidate these varied exposures into a single picture that accurately exposes the entire range of brightness.

32. Photograph for HDR

Effective HDR requires a series of photos, each at a different exposure. Many cameras can be set to take such a series, usually the three bracketed shots that are the effective minimum for HDR processing.

You may want a greater number of pictures covering a greater exposure range. The range should include proper exposures for both the brightest and darkest parts of the picture,

Turn off the camera's automatic features. This ensures that the camera doesn't induce unnecessary differences, such as changes in automatic exposure or focusing.

Ideally, you also should shoot from a tripod and stick to subjects that don't move. Adjustments within the HDR process can correct small variances in positioning and eliminate motion such as blowing leaves. Still, it works best to minimize these at the outset.

33. Start the program

You can start HDR Efex from Photoshop, Lightroom or Aperture.

Using Lightroom or Aperture

Start by importing the series of photos into Aperture or Lightroom. Then:

In Aperture, select the pictures. Then, make these menu selections:

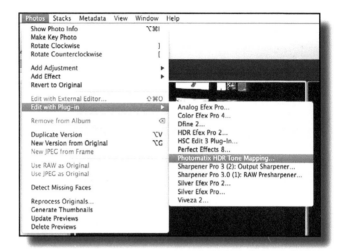

In Lightroom, after selecting the pictures, make these menu selections:

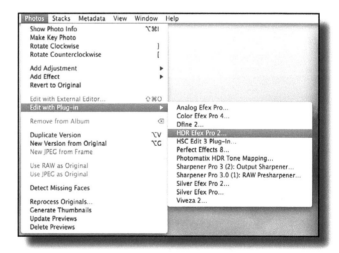

The process in Photoshop

In Photoshop, start by opening each file. Then, select:

A dialog box asks you to indicate the files you want to merge. If you have opened the files in Photoshop, you can simply select **Add Open Files**. You also have the option of selecting other files at this point.

Make your selections; then, click on **Merge Dialog**.

The merged picture opens in HDR Efex.

You can also check
the option of con-
ducting the merge as
a Photoshop smart
object.

34. Set alignment and bust ghosts

The first screen includes a dialog box with which you can set the terms of the eventual merger.

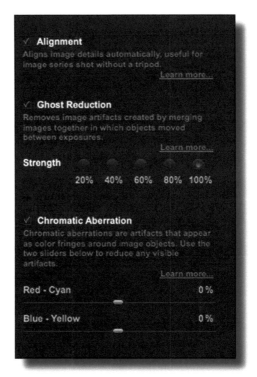

Normally, you can leave these as is, but there are times you might want to customize the process. You can check these options:

- **Alignment**. If you shot a series of hand-held exposures, chances are each exposure will be framed a little differently. Even tripod exposures can vary slightly. If you check this setting, the program will line up
  the exposures so they match exactly.

- **Ghost Reduction**. This option compensates for move-
  ment in the subject. Leaves may blow or, as happened
  once to me, my dog may wander into the scene. These

transient motions leave ghost-like traces. This setting tries to eliminate them (but didn't eliminate all traces of the dog).

- **Strength**. This sets the strength of the ghost reduction. Sometimes, ghost reduction will add artifacts instead of removing them. Reducing the strength can often correct this.

- **Chromatic Aberration** can correct color fringes introduced by the camera lens.

When ready, click on **Create HDR**. The final HDR screen opens.

35. Make the final mix

This screen provides tools to make the final mix of shading and other qualities. On the left is a panel of presets you can select to automatically apply selected settings to the final product.

On the right are detailed settings you can use to make precise, specific adjustments.

Probably the most effective use of this screen is to apply a preset that comes close to your desired result. Then, use the right-hand adjustments to refine the output.

Select a preset

Earlier HDR programs were notorious for adding a *grunge* effect to the picture. HDR Efex does not do this unless you want it. (See the **Surreal** presets.)

In the left-hand panel, the **Preset Library** is divided into several categories. The **Architecture** group might offer the best choices for this picture.

Select the preset that best suits your purpose.

Add a custom preset

Add a preset to the **Favorites** category by clicking on the star before its name.

You may create a combination of left- and right-panel settings that you want to save and use again. If so, you can save this combination as a custom preset.

With your selections in effect, click on the **Plus** sign on the **Custom** button. You are asked to provide a name for the preset. Enter it, and click on **OK**. The preset is now available under the **Custom** button.

Repeat history

The **History** button displays a history of presets and other settings you have applied to the current picture. You can click on any item to revert to that status.

36. Fine-tune the picture

The right-hand panel provides tools to help you fine-tune the picture. The five buttons here all lead to drop-down panels that offer multiple settings.

Tone compression

All these buttons also include reversion arrows you can use to undo any mistakes.

This is the main tool to increase or decrease the picture's dynamic range. It includes these settings:

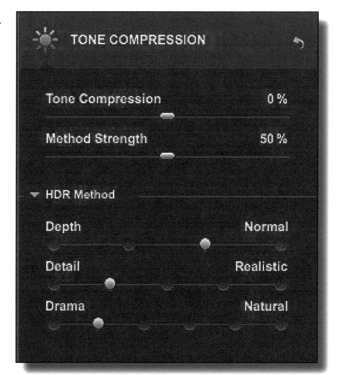

- **Tone compression**. This is the basic tool to adjust the dynamic range. Slide it to the right to darken bright areas and brighten those that are dark. Slide it to the left to do the opposite.

- **Method Strength**. This governs the strength of the

tone compression. Its main effect is on the amount of detail that appears in the image. Slide right to increase detail; left to decrease it.

- **HDR method**. You can use any combination of the three methods in this group.

- **Depth** can add visual dimension to the picture. Slide right to increase depth; left to reduce it or turn it off. This split screen shows the difference.

- **Detail**. This slide controls the amount of fine detail that appears. Settings range from Soft on the left to Grungy on the right.

Adjust the tone

The Tonality settings give you a chance to apply basic exposure and contrast settings to the completed picture.

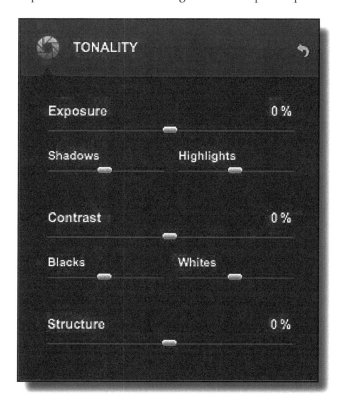

The **Exposure** and **Contrast** settings should be familiar. **Structure** is a NIK staple that adjust fine details.

Use the **Shadows** and **Highlights** sliders to increase or decrease the exposure in these areas. The **Blacks** and **Whites** sliders affect only the most extreme shades. Use them to recover details in these areas.

Adjust color

Three sliders in the Color section provide the means to correct problems with color rendition.

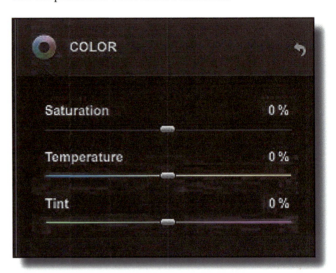

You can increase or decrease the saturation, adjust the overall temperature between warm and cool, and change the tint between green and magenta.

Selective adjustments

As with other NIK products, you can set control points to adjust selected parts of the picture.

For details of using
control points, see
*"3. Pointing with U
Point."*

For example, you might find the exterior view in this
picture is still a little too light. Set a control point in the
window; then decrease the exposure a little.

Finishing up

The **Finishing** section gives you three more options
for fine tuning the picture. These are available in other
photo editing applications, but it can be useful to have
them here.

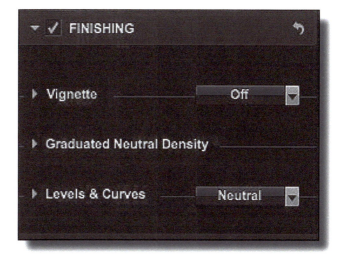

- **Vignette** corrects the tonal variations some camera lenses produce around the edges of the picture.

- **Graduated Neutral Density** emulates the camera filter that darkens an otherwise overexposed sky.

- **Levels and Curves** provides traditional means of setting color ranges and contrast.

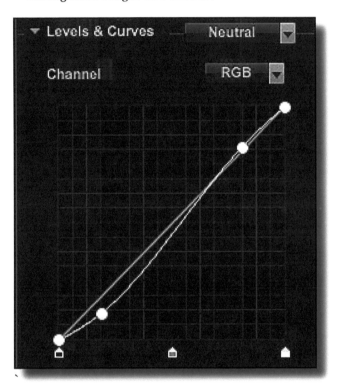

When all is finished, click on **Save** to preserve the processed picture.

Index